Solitude, Tarot & the Corona Blues

Solitude, Tarot & the Corona Blues

Poems by

Catherine Arra

© 2022 Catherine Arra. All rights reserved.
This material may not be reproduced in any form, published,
reprinted, recorded, performed, broadcast,
rewritten or redistributed without
the explicit permission of Catherine Arra.
All such actions are strictly prohibited by law.

Cover by Shay Culligan
Author photo by Jennifer B. Muirhead Photography

ISBN: 978-1-63980-240-1

Kelsay Books
502 South 1040 East, A-119
American Fork, Utah 84003
Kelsaybooks.com

Gratitude

To my publisher, Karen Kelsay, of Aldrich Press/Kelsay Books and the wonderful staff at the press.

To Cindy Hochman of "100 Proof" Copyediting Services for her masterful proofreading and treasured friendship.

To Tina Barry, Will Nixon, and Jo Pitkin for their generous words of praise.

To Tina Barry and Jo Pitkin, teaching artists at the Poetry Barn, whose workshops inspired and provided critique for many of the poems in this collection.

To Lissa Kiernan, founder and director of the Poetry Barn, and to the amazing community of poets online and at Second-Draft Sundays for their valuable feedback and critique.

To the Stone Ridge Library Writers for their steadfast commitment to a writing group, their honesty in offering critical feedback, and their patience through revisions.

Heartfelt gratitude to my friends and family who show up for readings, buy books, and promote my work.

Special thanks to my two soul sisters Beverly Bennett and Linda Harris for reading the many drafts and revisions, and for cooking, drinking, laughing, and crying with me. For being there, always.

Other Books by Catherine Arra

Deer Love
(2021)

*Her Landscape,
Poems Based on the Life of Mileva Marić Einstein*
(2020)

(*Women in Parentheses*)
(2019)

Writing in the Ether
(2018)

Tales of Intrigue & Plumage
(2017)

Loving from the Backbone
(2015)

Slamming & Splitting
(2014)

Acknowledgments

Grateful acknowledgment is made to the editors of the publications in which the following poems first appeared, sometimes in an earlier version:

First Literary Review-East: "Strength"

Hobo Camp Review: "Beauty in the Time of Corona"

Lothlorien Poetry Journal: "*Brinidsi*," "High on a Slanted Ceiling," "Ode to His Parrot," "The Sun," "The Tower," "Wheel of Fortune," "Writer's Block"

Muddy River Poetry Review: "Boomerang," "Corona Blues," "The Devil," "The Lovers," "The Moon"

Panoplyzine: "Table"

Propertius Press Poetry Anthology: Spheres and Canticles: "Second Seasons"

Pure Slush Friendship Anthology: "Cooking in the Time of Corona"

Rat's Ass Review: "Paradox"

Stone Poetry Journal: "The Summons"

Stone Poetry Journal: Gone, but Not Forgotten (An Anthology of Poems about Dead Pets): "Between Us and Them"

The Rye Whiskey Review: "Exodus," "Grief, a Hangover"

The Piker Press: "Badass," "Break Me," "The Fool," "The High Priestess"

Verse-Virtual: "Like Water," "Weeding"

Contents

Exodus	17
Table	18
Boomerang	19
Beauty in the Time of Corona	20
The Summer of Motherless Fawns	21
Like Water	23
Cooking in the Time of Corona	24
November	25
Break Me	26
Weeding	28
Paradox	30
Badass	31
The Other Pandemic	33
The Summons	34
Grief, a Hangover	35
Between Us and Them	36
Writer's Block	37
High on the Slanted Ceiling	38
Second Seasons	39
Ode to His Parrot	40
Corona Blues	41
Brindisi	43

The Tarot Poems

The Fool	47
The Magician	48
The High Priestess	50
The Empress	51
The Emperor	52
The Hierophant	53
The Lovers	54
The Chariot	55

Strength	56
The Hermit	57
Wheel of Fortune	59
Justice	60
The Hanged Man	62
Death	63
Temperance	64
The Devil	65
The Tower	66
The Star	67
The Moon	68
The Sun	69
Judgement	70
The World	71
Bibliography for the Tarot Poems	73–74
About the Author	75

All is fair in poetry and prose.

Exodus

And we went into the desert of quarantine.

Sat under Buddha's tree, faced the shadow of ourselves,
bright personas, grand schemes stripped of stage.

Some armed themselves, summoned gangs, gathered guns,
loaded words cruel as bullets, blind with blame.

Some laid punches of slight upon children, spouses,
kicked the dog for good measure, spit on the sidewalk.

Others summoned that swarthy stranger, traded secret
messages in coded dreams. Stopped waiting for happiness.

Said come now, sit at my table, eat, drink with me.
Share this space and story.

And we who would never have met, kissed with ancient longing,
history thick as blood, and fell, fell, fell in love.

Table

I command the room
in the center of the house,
framed by a broad French door.
Reclaimed wood, wormhole marred,
deep-sea green, and square.
Two chairs, north and south,
two placemats and

too many ghosts.

On me she's delivered
decades of meals,
decided her fortune and fate.

Over me she's belly-laughed,
argued, collapsed in tears,
traded a battalion of truth for lies.

With me she ponders,
warms leftover night in sun.
She wonders, writes,
whispers to wildlife,
sights a new deer path
and hones her instincts.

Today, head in hand,
her gaze like gauze,
she squints
to see the years ahead—
the dinners she will serve
the love she wants to make.

The crumbs she must discard
to wipe my surface clean.

Boomerang

Well, I'll tell you, 2-D ain't 3-D,
moonglow ain't sunlight,
scratch-n'-sniff ain't finger-licking,
virtual, no five-sense real.

I mean, she looked hot, fit the fantasy—
shimmery blond, sultry alto, foreign accent
and just how to place her pinky finger
to her lips like a porno doll.

She let me talk dirty, be sixteen again, let me
lure her into my wife-dumped wrecked den—
me drowning in memory of my ex, her smell
all over, and down there, pleasure-pot pink.

I never considered smell—
that reptile sense, sniffing out danger, death—
your essential run, get-the-hell-away gut scream.
Who'd a thought . . .

Well, I'll tell you, it's a revenge boomerang,
a brain Hula-Hoop, fooling cold-blooded instinct.
I got her to fly to me from the other side of the world,
said I'd marry her, take care of her.

The minute she stepped off the plane wearing
that WeChat pout, I got a whiff.
In the car, a wall of illusion-fermenting stink.
The dog whined. Cowered behind my seat.

At least he could still run.

Beauty in the Time of Corona

She walked four to five miles a day for a year.
A tally of Fitbit steps. Over 1,600 miles of leaving him,

the marriage, wrestling through memory,
nettle, snags, swamp, drizzle, frigid gusts
stinging tears and more tears
until she was drenched with weeping.

Then Corona came and she walked to ask earth forgiveness—

Sandhill cranes in squawking mating dances.
Golden-necked anhinga winking her turquoise eye.
Sun streaming through fence slats. Wind on water palettes, sand.
Purple field grasses watercolor-washing the sky.

And that sky . . . all drama and God-gushing glory.

A reminder to look up. Beyond. Believe in cosmic clarity,
a full moon. Saturn conjunct Jupiter, how restrictions expand us.
In convergences. Transformation.
Walking . . . walking . . . to discover beauty in resilience.

Walking to track where she's been. Where she's going.

To walk to the belly of the Catskills. To the deer that live with her.
The beauty in belonging to herself. Home.

The Summer of Motherless Fawns

First it killed the elderly, then robust bucks,
mature does, leaving yearlings and spring fawns,
still camouflaged in spots, to find their way, alone.
EHD (Epizootic Hemorrhagic Disease). Deer Covid.

A virus carried by biting midges, coaxed
by climate change—relentless rain, humidity,
a swamp-soggy summer turning the Northeast into
a Petri dish for fungi and insects delivering disease.

Efficient, fast, fatal. A furious fever, mouth blisters.
Excessive salivation foams and beards bewildered
faces nosing into birdbaths to drink, cool, find relief
but finding none. 24–36 hours later, death wins.

The sick stumble in heavy-headed delirium, detach
from families, the herd. Nursing fawns follow
to groom, soothe, stay close to dazed mothers,
are left unrecognized, rejected, confused.

The dying come at dusk, in the gray between
life and death, between my species and theirs.
They know me as spirit mother, the woman
in the wood with apples, corn, and feral love.

I kneel before each one.
First, 8-point Nico. Then easygoing Gus
and little Enzo. New mother Zoe, old Hildy
and last, lovely Lacey—all the deer I know by name.

We speak the language of eye, ear, head movements,
of breaths, snorts, body postures.
Sullen, still, they gaze at me, asking,
What's happening? Why? Can you, will you, help?

But they've come to say goodbye,
to show themselves one last time.
To each I say a prayer of gratitude
for their company, for peace in their passage.

I stay until they turn into the wood,
into falling darkness like spirits
leaving earth on All Hallows' Eve
to become the bones of spring.
A herd of 30–40, now less than 15.
Rotting flesh fowls the air, buzzards circle.
Young females, one yearling, and
one old buck remain.

Hardwired instinct bonds fawns—
an orphan family of surrogate mothers
take turns grooming, coddling, comforting
to give each other shelter from abandonment.

I wonder, will they make it through,
never knowing the hunt, the snow, ice,
the sunken-belly want of winter—
my motherless fawns.

Like Water

in a rock well, whirlpooling
out a pinhole at the granite base—emptying
the way New York City empties the Ashokan
with flushing, showers, with waste and wanting,

I keep the old towns—foundations of homes,
stores, churches—visible in summer's drought.
Places we ate, chatted, made love, prayed,
before the 1905 project—before bulldozers
and floods for a reservoir in the womb-like basin
of the Catskills—for a city I'd never see.

I am that voluptuous basin
filled with fish, feeding eagles, bear,
climbing stone walls, spilling over,
traversing aqueducts, tunnels,
rocking driftwood, marooned boats,
flowing from the cellar
of the house where I stored jams, cured meats,
the rooms where I lived with a husband, four babies

—before tweed suits with money bargained, bought,
moved Grandma and the rest of the cemetery
to higher ground.

A marker at water's edge
says we lived here . . .
the towns of Brown's Station, Olive City,
Broadhead's Bridge, Ashton.

I am water. The keeper.

Cooking in the Time of Corona

for Beverly, Linda, Marian

Four women, longtime friends
make a pod for stability, company,
predictability like four points
on a compass, the four elements,
four seasons and navigate
Coronavirus peaks, spikes, and spread.

They take turns cooking for each other—
      succulent grilled lobster tails
      with cilantro butter
      an array of tapas
      pierogi, dumplings
      zucchini fritters, savory seafood skewers
      teriyaki-pineapple chicken, pastas
      sweet bites and oh-so-luscious
      flourless chocolate cake.

Giada, Ina, Martha would-be-proud meals
with good wine, mojitos, martinis, maybe prosecco,
tablescapes and elegance.

Artist, poet, teacher, dancer
unmask and sing "Happy Birthday"
celebrate another season and wait.

Witches in the wisdom of friendship
they drink too much, tell secret stories, dance
and make videos only they will ever see.

November

I

You die with fanfare and flourish,
scream crimson, cadmium yellow, coral.
Shocking my senses, you augur an end.

For the loss of you I mourn,
dreading the season of verticals and alabaster.
What a fool I am

to mistake a promise made
of such sweeping barefaced color and light
for the husband of broken gold.

II

She likes early morning,
not yet day, no longer night.
Alone in the impasse of dawn, when she's
not yet driven, no longer haunted.

When she sees beyond mist and dew,
past black bark silhouettes, through
blended ribs of sun and moon.
When she is the nature that is hers.

Break Me

Your text this morning:
I def. have Covid.
But I knew.

You, defiant warrior, would deliver
yourself to this crusade. Kept bar-lounging,
ski-lodging, trekking into cities
open-faced, blue bandana mask a ruse.
Kept on until biology bedded you.

And then, maybe you wanted this fight . . .
until you were in it:
101 temp, body aches, the whole 9 yards.

Sometimes, rugged one,
we derail ourselves
when we don't like the path we're on
and can't find a way off.
When we need to rest
and don't know how.
When we challenge nature
middle-finger the universe
because we don't much like ourselves.

Is that what you did?

Did you want something bigger than you,
your ambition, your shattered heart,
to burn away the shell of hard muscle
and Rambo resolve?
To bring yourself to your knees
before the tenderness you long for?

Don't you know,
you can't spar with yourself
and win?

Go on now, kneel
with sword, cross, snake in hand
and surrender.

Weeding

This morning's walk
the length of Vincent Lane
across the main road
into the cemetery, where
I go to weed the flowers
at my mother's gravesite,
a funeral procession.

Thirty or more cars lined along
the entranceway—sun hats, umbrellas
suits and flowers, bodies merging
to attend the end.

I do not have the verve to
disturb this last prayer and penance.

Turn back.

I think about how he said,
"Don't be disappointed in me," meaning
because I can't love you
or anyone again,
because I have been buried
in a sarcophagus of loss and
prefer to live with ghosts,
because I don't want to fail again,
because your disappointment
will remind me how disappointed I am
in myself.

In my silent stride home, I say
We all land in this final hiding place,
guarding inert bones,
a bloodless heart
with an eternal yearning
to make it beat again.

Paradox

We walked through war-zone destruction
to renovate Old Broadway.
We walked steadfast, serene
through jackhammers, backhoes, noise.

To renovate Old Broadway
our lives, dead marriages, torn-up love.
We walked steadfast, serene
moving forward, looking ahead, matching strides.

Our lives, dead marriages, torn-up love.
You reached for my hand, folded fingers into fingers
moving forward, looking ahead, matching strides.
And then, you let go.

You reached for my hand, folded fingers into fingers
reliving the past, refitting a future, matching strides.
And then, you let go.
Cracking concrete. The terror of touch.

Reliving the past, refitting a future, matching strides
I reached for your hand, smoothed palms, folded fingers.
Cracking concrete. The terror of touch.
Again, you let go.

I reached for your hand, smoothed palms, folded fingers
looking forward, matching strides, moving ahead.
Again, you let go.
I said, "You don't like to hold hands?"

Looking forward, matching strides, moving ahead.
Silence, silence, silence. Jackhammers. Backhoes. Noise.
I said, "You don't like to hold hands?"
Midway, midstride on Old Broadway, a dead end.

Badass

Has a bad case of the shorts
if you know what I mean . . .
short-changed, short-sighted, surly aggressive short guy.

Has an opinion about everything.
Is a life member of the mansplaining club,
most likely a Proud Boy too.

Badass has multiple Facebook pages, Instagram,
Twitter accounts, website w/blog and YouTube links.
Promotes his profound manhood, boy obsessions.

Shows off his guns, drums, and latest prey—usually
a catch-and-release largemouth bass—
all undercover as "writer."

Badass delivers his decrees, videos his diatribes as if he were
the finger of God, posts his daily exercise routines
from Sunday squats to 3-mile jogs—a real Rocky Balboa.

Badass knows it all and is, of course, a real pussy magnet,
so he thinks, with enough wails and whines about women
to send any good orgasm packing.

Badass is always the victim,
put upon by government, employers, rules of any kind,
wives, girlfriends, Alexa, but mostly other men with balls.

Badass thinks he's funny,
sucker punches for fun, then says *lighten up,
get a sense of humor.*

Badass is self-sabotage, ruined marriages,
failed affairs, and bar fights.
Badass figures best to pre-empt the diss before he's fingered—

just another frustrated middle-aged guy constipated with gripes and grievances, haunted by mediocrity, erasure, lost love.

Blog on, blog on, mighty man. Blog on.

The Other Pandemic

He died in the second season of Corona
never to hear Biden declared president,
so sure the man was daft and
Trumpian braggadocio would bully on.

We argued and hadn't spoken
since the first debate when
he let his politics out of the bag—
the sequestered silence of four years broken.

He slammed his palm on the countertop
like a judge's gavel to silence me, as if
I were still the little girl he punished
and sent to her room.

He must have thought he'd live forever—
89 years old, 20% heart function, on oxygen.
Never saw the exploding lung clot coming
until it did.

1,800 miles away, I had hoped he'd call
in the last weeks of his expiring life.
He died in the second season of Corona,
never to hear his only daughter's voice again.

The Summons

Tonight, I will dream you back to my childhood,
to the room at the end of the hall.
I'll find you hammering down Sheetrock,
a sweaty silhouette in a jagged white hole.
I'll stand in the doorway to witness your work and tell you
how my breasts couldn't grow in that room,
how dancing under the eaves, I always bumped my head.

I'll show you how I learned to live in the middle because
you liked me that way, because you never had the time
to renovate or the stomach for unboundaried spaces.
I'll remind you how you would have burned me
at the bedpost, rubbed my nose in fear I peed
with the puppy had I asked or needed, and I did need
more, like the man-strength to hammer down walls.

I'll see again the skies I painted on each low eave,
the moon in its phases, the sun lifting apricot clouds.
I'll remember how Mother defied you and permitted
them to stay, though six coats of paint wouldn't cover
the mess when I finally moved out—still, it bled through.
I've heard you tell that story with an annoyed chuckle
to remind me of the chore of fatherhood.

But tonight, I will tell my stories and you will work
until you have listened and I have forgiven you, released you
after the decades of men I've loved to finally love you.

Tonight, I will summon you back.
By the force of my need, you will make a portal
and give me leave of this room once more and for all.

Grief, a Hangover

Circular, circuitous. Unmapped.

Requires kegs of time, ten-toed tightroping
to miss the wall, skip the fall, gutter-banging brains.

You can't lose the headache, crotch ache,
the heavy-footed hungover hunger. The loss.

You stagger grocery aisles, drive snail-pace slow in
your own funeral procession, horns honking behind.

Cursed and dazed, you move in sludge.

You think you are speeding. You almost want the cliff
to arrow into space, hang glide down.

Weightless, aloft, free.

But you keep on. Keep on chasing ghosts,
feeding pain, order another bourbon.

One more shot won't make a difference
any more than one more phone call, one more kiss.

One more roll under the sheets of delusion.

It will be better this time, you say.
But it never is, no matter how tight you hold the pen,

the wish, the full-throttle control of authorship.
You can't rewrite the story.

Between Us and Them

a blizzard today, the first of winter,
late for even the groundhog.

I've braised a hearty stew, baked a pumpkin pie.
He spent daybreak writing, now naps.

Perhaps this fourth season, frantic
and silent, will help us mend a new fracture,
swallow the rawness again.

This time not a father, a grandmother. A dog,
Kugie, broken in a squirrel chase. The car
unable to stop its red or the death howl.

He's only a dog, we know.
Panama and Jemmie only cats. It's only snow,
this blizzard.

The white will melt and give way, gather us in drifts,
freeze until spring when we will know better

how to live in two houses
and run between them a snowy bridge.

Writer's Block

I don't know what to do
when you submit to her, strip yourself down
to a miscued hard-on, let her ram it straight into your brain.

I don't know how to warn you against the seduction
or the indolence she induces.

I know she invented black garters and lace,
is an expert at choked-up cleavages.

I know there's a trick to cracking whips
and coaxing death before it's time.

How do I tell you, better to suffer
the suffering of muted words?

How can I ask you to imagine finished pages
or convince you Penelope waits
while Circe screws you over?

High on the Slanted Ceiling

A reflection shimmers like a tear in satin,
a rip in the tapestry of Sunday morning ease.

Magnified molecules and gaseous swirls
of another landscape find us in the folds of our flesh.

Your lava silvers my belly, sliding to indigo sheets,
crisp by your making our bed ready for bluer waves.

We carry low in our bowels. And though your sex rests
thigh-cushioned and sated, swollen in a ruddy glow,

and I, drowsy in scents, nestle under your chin,
we are stirred into the lens with sun and water.

The helioscope of sensation ends, hearing last, the echo
of an orgasm, a sigh, we go from fingertips

alone through the portal.

Second Seasons

In ravaged soil, where too many forsythia
grew—a tangled web of strangling roots
a snaky nest of untended vines—

let us plant a garden now, where sun was
forbidden, clapboards rotted from lack of air.

Let us lift tired sod in wrinkled hands
sift it through the till of fingers
turn and knead it like children making mud pies.

Massage it to feeling
give it back to itself.

Let us choose the best of our seasons:
coneflowers, phlox, dahlias, and daisies
tall shoots, dwarfs, spikes, and cushions.

Let us grow tomato plants, long and lacy
with backbones strong by the green of their making.

In distilled grace, let us plant a garden for
regret, sorrow, forgiveness, tend the past in beginnings.

Let us make a place to rest on porch-rocking evenings
hand in hand, the sweet juice of tomatoes
dribbling down our chins.

Ode to His Parrot

Lilac-crowned, ruby-nosed
tufted iridescent green

how you'd have been a star
at the rainforest gala

if ever you hatched in nest
beneath belly feathers and coos

in sultry nights
soft rains

before hungry boys snatched
you for a dollar.

Poached, packed, parceled
incubated for pet-store prowlers

you landed in his cage
the one meant for me as ultimatum.

His house, his rules, he lost
and you, poor Polly, gazed at winter

shivered, screeched, cawed, clawed
and crapped on his rug

instead of me.

Corona Blues

By the close of Covid-19
on the brink of Delta V,
runaway husband, bandit with parrot
on a quest for new exciting love,
returned—tail-tattered & shipwrecked,
knocking . . .
        She felt his pain.

Cool writer-dude turned out
to be a counterfeit copycat,
caged by his not-so-clever thievery.
        She felt sorry for him,
           how he squandered his talent.

Facebook predators
in disguised despair, paltry poetry,
seductive food pics, Daliesque portraits,
requested her friendship, messaged sweet spam.
        She felt fake like them.
        Avatars of noir, mystique, hard muscle.

Who are you? she'd write.
Who are you?
Bang. Bang. Blocked.

She paddled her Corona canoe up & downriver,
masked & unmasked, vaxed & vexed.
She cooked, wrote, streamed, strolled, & ran.
She executed a ballet of yoga poses.
She drank, got drunk, cried, slept it off,
& did it all again. She emptied a lake of rum.

She capsized,
prayed & died with wildlife.

She dove into the Torah of Tarot.
Tail-tattered & shipwrecked, she summoned
the avatars of humanity for help.
    She swam her way home.

Brindisi

Sweet dance of my life
be graceful as the gilded wake
of white pelicans

Forging a fierce faith
into morning solitude
opening portals

Of connectedness
spontaneous embraces
unmasked joy seated

With local honey
wedge of brie, chilled prosecco
after-Covid tea.

The Tarot Poems

The Fool

I am the jester-joker,
colorful and carefree.
I am the wayward vagabond, gypsy-bum
come to tempt you, tease you,
take you away.

I am zero, the beginning,
the sum of none.
White spaces, black holes,
the emptiness before conception,
silence before sound,
the undivided stillness before a storm.

I am twilight—which one, you decide.

Anything can happen in my grasp
and grasp I do—catch you unawares
when days have grown weary,
desire dull.

You'll never know on which shoulder I'll land,
in which ear I'll whisper.

I am your innocence, your puppy-dog instinct,
your waiting satchel, the perfect white rose.
I say, Come. Come this way
with your child's mind and reckless abandon.

I am your laughter and acquiescence,
your surrender to faith or folly.
I dance you along a precipice,
my fool in tow, take you
to the edge, to the daunting fall,
where you alone must choose
to leap or turn.

The Magician

Far from my playful predecessor, impulsive jester
who stirs the pot, prompts a laugh, initiates a quest—

I am you arrived at your table, our tools for alchemy
ready at the quick.

We are the artist, entrepreneur emerging,
the bridge between seen and unseen,
the wand that manifests.

I am you in hours of writing, painting,
composing, inventing. Those holy hours when morning is
suddenly afternoon, hunger forgotten.

I am the magic in Einstein's thought experiments,
O'Keeffe's visions, Mozart's octave madness,
Dickinson's cadence.

I am the power
that harnesses, delivers.

I am the recipe perfected, the garden designed,
the house built, the child reared—
all you have taken from the ether and sculpted into form.

The work, the original work
of your life.

I am the tunnel you must travel
by sheer mastery of will to become the vessel
that births what did not exist before.

But beware, my brave Houdini,
the gifts of miracle and deception are manifold—
the manipulation of elements never to be abused.

Look, look here—
follow my gold coin there.

You may discover radium, unfold the formula
for nuclear fusion, and so be the one who gives
the order to kill millions.

The High Priestess

No need for a crystal ball
or pendulum.
No palmist, priest, or priestess.

The map
of your history, destiny
your feminine knowing
floats between fluttering lashes
winks behind violet lace
in ripples, whispers
in eventide, solitude, dreams.

Defer to voicelessness,
defy logic.
Glide green seawater
dive brackish depths.
Swim with octopi and urchins.

Abide by moonlight.
Move only with tides.

The Empress

I'm the bloody mess
from which you emerged—
seeds, swamp-loam
forests, fertility.

I'm unfurled flesh
bone-burrowing urgency
the whale-splash arrival
with gestation and guts. Your first gasp.

Travel backward to know me
first as huntress, warrior, lover—
Diana, Athena, Venus.
I sustain your journey as earth and sea.

Honor me as Demeter, Hestia, Hera
the Madonna, and know prosperity, abundance
harvest, home. Without me, endless winter
the blank page, a blighted muse.

As witch, crone, sorceress, salvation,
bow before me or squander in
penniless poverty, stumble moonless nights,
die in a loveless bed.

I am mother, the garden
beyond Eve. As I made you with the seed
of my king, I can smother and drown you.
I am the belly of the world.

The Emperor

I shaped your first image of a man,
your bond to other men, women,
your own authority.

Maybe you despised me,
now hate the boss and
woe to anyone who crosses you—

women who ignore your
fits and fury, unruly children,
men who laugh at your posturing.

Maybe you adored me,
model me, help a neighbor change a tire,
read bedtime stories, cook dinner—

the father who let you become
artist, carpenter, soldier, lawyer,
gay, straight, bi, or trans.

I am necessary either way.
Without me you falter,
butterfly flits, hits the windshield, flattens.

Too much of me is
strength without flexibility,
trigger-finger tyranny.

Too little of me is
an untended garden
weed-choked and barren.

Yes, I make the rules.
I am trains that run on time,
plans that work.

The Hierophant

I'm far from poetry,
no whimsy, free-verse frivolity here.
I'm the rule book, formula, the predictable plot.

I'm rites of passage
the seven sacraments, ceremony.
I'm the recipe for success, connect-the-dots art.

I'm robed education, degrees, doctrines,
the creed, code, academy,
the triple-crowned tiara of acceptance.

I'm the priest, Pope, therapist, professor,
boot-camp sergeant for the masses,
tour guide for spirit.

I'm not for the traveler who stays the course alone.

But beware, beware, my faithful fans,
I, too, am delirious dogma
in the holy hunger to belong, right or wrong.

The cult, evangelical, born-again QAnon.
The oligarch, demigod, the one who corrupts, molests,
hides, lies in the folds of his cassock.

This I say to you who kneel before me:
Remember, Jesus was Jewish jazz.

The Lovers

I am that wicked triangle.
You between two strange angels,
Eve or Lilith, good boy or naughty other.
I tease desire, make you sweat.

I stand opposite The Devil
in a do-si-do of sacred and profane.
Good angel and fallen one, we are
twins of choice, a tempting cocktail.

Choose one, never know the other,
but choose you must. Indecision
is the dead-end loop cowards circle—
the heart's crossroads,

urging, beguiling . . . go right, left
or straight ahead.
Be earthbound or free,
seduced or loved.

The Chariot

I am your red Corvette, Jeep,
Tesla, truck, compact or sedan . . .

your body, your ride,
the Ben-Hur fire and grit
to travel long, wide, to arrive.

I am the force
of your personality, the sass

to surrender childhood, untangle
adolescence—defy the curfew,
write your own rules

to know the lure
of a first kiss, choose
how you will love.

I am the road trip,
your life's work, the torque
by which it is mapped.

How will you go, mighty charioteer?
With determination, restraint?
Or in reckless drunk fun?

How will you care for me,
for others?

Take up the reins, steer the course,
set your trajectory.

You alone harness
good and evil, stay the goal,
arrive in triumph or defeat.

Strength

To know the beast within—a familiar spirit.
What is yours?

Greet your gorgeous Bandersnatch,
your fang-toothed fear.

Gather sexual frisson, animal fright,
quell the instinct to strike.

Gather wildness, your first true nature
into hands of compassion, gentle intent.

Open the mouth that snarls,
find the courage that is grace.

The Hermit

I am your solitude, the voice
you recognize as your own.

I am lamp
and lamplighter,

the hooded figure on a cliff,
candle in a cave.

I am the one who
gathers vision into one eye,

sees your genesis,
fuses all into a beacon

for you,
who think you travel alone.

You, who listen
for counsel, secrets of prophets,

for connection to all things
before and after you.

I welcome you to your single path
among the many that lead to me.

I am the old wise man
you see in the eyes of elephants,

the answer in wordless prayers.

I am Jesus, Buddha, Brahma,
Moses, Allah, Odin.

I am the top of the mountain
and the guide.

I am the *namaste*.

Wheel of Fortune

The inevitable arrives on time,
never when you're ready.

The figures on your carousel
rise and fall.

Seasons shimmy into years,
wrinkles furrow brows, claw eyes,

Fortune is arbitrary,
a marble ricochets off the roulette wheel.

I am not cause and effect,
that dreaded karma loop.

Your effort and actions
do not concern me

any more than gravity cares for
planets held in orbit.

I happen without you.
You happen in me.

Go up, go down, move with me
or resist. Control is illusion.

From my whirling hub, on spokes of
uncertainty, chaos, chance,

you will spin in cycles
on blurs of silver.

Justice

You see, I have no expression
of approval or disapproval,
no smile or sneer.

I do not judge or punish. I'm not
concerned with mathematical exactness,
an eye for an eye, innocence or guilt.

I sit midway between heaven and earth,
man's law and spiritual law.
Before me, all have equal standing.

For you, I mediate, adjust,
hold the scales to measure
the weight of polarities:

love–hate, good–evil, pleasure–pain,
the seesaw of your morality, the cause
and effect of action.

I give you the sword of sacrifice
to correct, restore, to sustain sobriety,
find truth in balance. To understand:

loneliness is selfishness returned,
impotence, the failure to be present in love,
stinginess, a poverty of spirit.

All opposites unite in me,
merge into harmony
as they must in you.

I am the equality of opposition,
gravity in the orbit of extremes.
I am the end of separation

when a single soul
and the world soul
become one.

The Hanged Man

Go now, climb that tree.
Hook your left leg on a sturdy branch,
cross the other over your knee into a triangle.

Clasp your hands on the small of your back,
your arms two more triangles, making three,
and hang backward.

Heart above head, the world upside down,
how long can you stay in this suspended state
like monarchs in milkweed?

Will you accept reversals, altered angles,
surrender or resist? Can you wait in self-sacrifice,
your chosen crucifixion?

Death

I am the chrysalis of your molting,
a cradle of stardust, moonlight, spider threads,
and memory.

I am loss. Mother, Father, self,
the breakup, car crash, abandonment,
betrayal.

I am the ending that begins, the sequestered space
between . . . the embryo.
I am new love, a child, new home.

My arrival is sudden, though I lurk
on the rim of desire, the tips of eyelashes
unseen. (You knew I was coming.)

The shock of me slams the senses,
accelerates time, slows you to stasis, spins you
into my truss.

The cycle of your days blurs
identities of lifetimes.
All judgments and rebirths coalesce.

Stripped of flesh, you segue the end
of this story to the next on skeleton feet,
the rhythm of your bones a new beat

thrumming, drumming
to bring you home
again, to me.

Temperance

One foot in water, the other on earth,
I transfer pathos between goblets, one to the other,
the other to one, spill and fill, spill and fill.

Call me your fountain, the flow of your temperament,
the tug-of-war in tidal surges, impulse in undertow.
I can bring you home or shipwreck you.

Sway in my ebb, my flow, rock
in equanimity, a little of this, some of that,
reconcile *bitch* and *bastard*.

Find tightrope balance, the recipe
that nourishes.
Wait when you want to run.

I am the yield sign, the bartender
who cuts you off, the seat belt.
I slow your hurtling heart.

I pace the push and pull, prevent the overspill
and fall. I holster the gun, write
the peace treaty.

Like the hub of the Wheel of Fortune, I am
you in stillness, balance in turbulence,
sight in the cyclone center.

Not fate but the water wheel within
that tempers the molten metal
in your fiery forge.

The Devil

I'm your badass bully bitch, the one you don't much like,
the shadow sulking behind smiles.

I poke, provoke, have you roped,
harnessed by the balls, breasts, your deep-throated guilt.

I am you rejected, you unseen, the one you
want to love, the angel you deny.

I'm the big bad metaphor,
Lucifer, Mephistopheles, vampire hunger.

Addictions, obsessions, one-night stands,
sensation severed from understanding.

I manipulate in stealth, steal who you are,
call others the you that is me.

Don't be ashamed or shame me.
I'm the terrified child, lost, alone, hiding in you.

Embrace me now. Kiss my scorched lips,
stroke my bestial belly and wild bat wings.

Heal my broken heart, take me home.
To love me is to release me.

The Tower

You've been told a thousand times:
Castles without foundations fall.
Flesh devoid of spirit is dead.

I let you have at it long enough.
Watched you betray your best friend,
steal his wife.
Watched you squander the inheritance
of your father's sweat.
Take without permission,
take for granted.

In love with the avatar
you jazzed up for yourself,
you never saw me coming.

I'm the storm
in your 50th year,
the lightning strike
market crash, the affair.
The pandemic, diagnosis,
the knock on the door that
alters your life forever.

I'm the change you didn't invite
to the party, embrace in bed.
The change necessary, but you refused.
Gave the power of choice to me.

I'm your bad behavior come back to you,
your life in the red.
I'm one decisive stroke to zero.

The Star

You've wished upon me all your life.
*Twinkle, twinkle . . . how I wonder
. . . above the world . . . a diamond . . .*

Yet your wish is to find
me in yourself, to radiate promise,
be a balm in bitterness.

I am blessing and beacon as
Christmas star, North Star,
Venus, Jupiter, Mars.

I am the diamond
of you in this delicate life,
your third-eye insight.

I am the urge to look up.

When you lose me
in fog, stumble,
seek excess to numb doubt,

when despair stalks you,
disease finds you, pessimism sleeps
you through days,

I float Milky Way nights—

a star's reach to your constellation,
all you can become.
Go ahead, wish.

Wish upon me tonight.

The Moon

Mistress of nightshades,
guardian of cats, owls, wolves,
sea creatures and water worlds.

In dreams, fantasy, tides, and blood cycles
I entice you to lose your way, make you
shatter me in a cruel casting of stones
on mirrored water, watch you submit as I ripple
to wholeness again and again.

Night vision portal, floating white orb, pregnant
with secrets, deceptions, the longings
you tell no one.

I answer the faith you bestow in gazing upon me,
calling my names:

Wolf in the howling hunger of January.
Worm when earth softens and sap flows.

Strawberry when night air sweetens.
Buck for velvet antlers crowning kings.

Harvest for abundance.
Blue for your lost twin.

I am the seasons of your psyche.
I carry you to fullness, erase you in darkness.

Teach you to trust what cannot be seen.

The Sun

I am salacious yellow
spilling myself across your table,
your face, after weeklong rain,
winter's waste, the darkest nights.

I make you squint,
wear shades, but
you look me in the eye
fall into my arms, say,

Yes, yes, yes to my light,
my offering, my joy, to the wonder
of childhood lost, the playground buried,
to happiness in reprise.

I am peach juice silking lips, sunflowers
looking upward, folded wishes reflected
in rippling water, answered.
The better day with or without clouds.

I am love returned, love renewed.
I am the original you
before storms and famine
quakes and floods, nightmares and doubt.

I am you come home
to you as light.

Judgement

I'm the bullet or the miss,
the ticket or the passport denied.
That Christian thing, too . . .
heaven or hell.

I'm the reckoning. The duel.

Dues paid, debts settled,
you're free to go, choose your next
story. The World awaits.

Go on, sing the song of yourself
with fiddles and drums, click your heels,
toss your hat high. Say farewell to
mirrored mirages.

Walk through the shimmer.

I anoint you with forgiveness, fortune,
with flight from the lie you fed yourself,
from the dead ones who'd keep you dead—

those who sleep the slumber of flesh,
die in carcasses of doubt, praying
for relief. But you made the trek
to me, your angel.

Parked the ego, put lust and mistrust
in the back seat, left the race.
I'm your afterlife in life.

You were lost and now you're found . . .
as the song goes.
I am that amazing benevolent grace.
I am you delivered.

The World

When you find yourself with me,
androgynous dancer, wreathed in laurel,
framed by the four elements, poised
in the ballet of alchemy,

you have climbed the mountain
of your foolish self, lost your
way on meandering paths, slipped
in mud, slept in rain.

You scaled each elevation hand over hand
passed players who sabotaged your compass,
tripped you in turbulence, trapped
you in temptation.

You footed each new plateau, breathless,
heart pounding a warrior's beat, exploding
chest space, pulsing vibrations into aura,
into ether, to align your little life in mine.

I am The World,
life that transcends and takes you.
Your reward is this vista,
to see eternity, your truest self.

To understand you are dancing stardust
on a cosmic stage.

Bibliography for the Tarot Poems

As a teenager, I developed a fascination with the tarot, and then as a literature major in college, with the archetypes. I later delved into Jungian psychology and the archetypes of the collective unconscious. As an English and creative writing teacher, I encouraged my students to find and interpret symbols, archetypes, patterns, and motifs in literature as well as in their own writing.

The tarot poems in this collection are a natural progression of my original interest in the cards and my personal belief in spirit and intuitive foretelling. For the poems, I consulted the tarot sources listed below and then integrated my background, my reading and study, with my own intuitive understanding of the mighty symbols of the Major Arcana. You may agree or disagree with my interpretations. Either way, thanks for reading.

~Catherine

Adam, Elliot. *Fearless Tarot*. Woodbury, MN., Llewellyn Publications, 2020.

Connolly, Eileen. *Tarot, The New Handbook for the Apprentice*. Franklin Lakes, NJ, New Page Books, 1979.

Connolly, Eileen. *Tarot, The Handbook for the Journeyman*. North Hollywood, CA, New Castle Publishing Co. Inc., 1987.

Crispin, Jessa. *The Creative Tarot, A Modern Guide to an Inspired Life*. New York, NY, Touchstone / Simon & Schuster, 2016.

Dean, Liz. *The Golden Tarot*. London / New York, CICO Books, 2008.

Gray, Eden. *The Complete Guide to the Tarot.* New York, NY, Bantam Books, Crown Publishers Inc., 1970.

Gong, Tina. *Tarot.* New York, NY, DK Publishing, 2020.

Nichols, Sallie. *Jung and Tarot, An Archetypal Journey.* York Beach, ME, Samuel Weiser Inc., 1980.

About the Author

Catherine Arra is a former high school English and writing teacher. Since leaving the classroom in 2012, her poetry and prose have appeared in numerous literary journals online and in print, and in several anthologies. She is the author of *Deer Love* (Dos Madres Press, 2021), *Her Landscape, Poems Based on the Life of Mileva Marić Einstein* (Finishing Line Press, July, 2020), (*Women in Parentheses*) (Kelsay Books, 2019), *Writing in the Ether* (Dos Madres Press, 2018), and three chapbooks: *Tales of Intrigue & Plumage* (FutureCycle Press, 2017), *Loving from the Backbone* Flutter Press, 2015), and *Slamming & Splitting* (Red Ochre Press, 2014). Arra is a native of the Hudson Valley in upstate New York, where she lives most of the year, teaches part-time, and facilitates local writing groups. In winters she migrates to the Space Coast of Florida. Find her at www.catherinearra.com.

www.ingramcontent.com/pod-product-compliance
Lightning Source LLC
Chambersburg PA
CBHW030913170426
43193CB00009BA/831